GW00514807

Dogs Are Funny

A Bark & Smile™ Book

Kim Levin

Andrews McMeel
Publishing

Kansas City

ISBN: 0-7407-1048-6

Library of Congress Catalog Card Number:
00-100444

www.barkandsmile.com

For Christine

Acknowledgments

I want to acknowledge all of the funny dogs in this book, along with their owners. This book is dedicated to Christine, my best friend, who is and has always been the funniest person I know. Special thanks to everyone at Andrews McMeel Publishing who shares my love of dogs and the humor they bring to our lives.

Introduction

Dogs are just plain funny. Of all the amazing qualities that dogs have, and there are so many, the one that truly touches me is their ability to brighten any moment. I photograph dogs, in particular, because I have always had this incredible bond with each dog I meet, and they always make me laugh. I find something humorous in each dog I photograph. And most important, dogs have this uncanny ability to bring out the funny side in all of us.

Dogs are funny
because . . .

they laugh

they wear sweaters

they ride in wagons

they're clumsy

they roll in the grass

they cock their heads

they sit for cookies

they howl

they can touch their
tongues to their noses

they have funny faces

they pant

they stand on two feet

they have big heads

they reminisce

they eat shoes

they play peekaboo

they're fluffy

they're happy

they lean

they get wet

they play tug-of-war

they rule the city

they get stuck

they grin

they eat Frisbees

they have big ears

they question

they chew

they wear socks

they play quarterback

they run wild and free

they dress up

they yawn

they amuse themselves
(and us)

they just plain
look funny